I dedicate this book to my amazing daughter. She used to ride around with me in my truck while I was trying to market my first business. Even though at the time, when I was frustrated and felt like a zero, I was still her biggest hero. Years later, after learning the art of adding zeros, she has become a power-house of one; an immovable object of determination coupled with an unstoppable force of success. To this day, she still teaches me the value of true wealth. I could not be more proud, and would not be who I am without her in my life. I LOVE YOU THIIIIIIS MUCH!

PREFACE

Do you know that moment, when you're holding an ice-cold beer and twisting off the cap? There's that slight resistance… then, pssst and you're enjoying that sweet, sweet nectar. I'm assuming a lot here; you're old enough to drink, you actually drink and you like beer. Nonetheless, I'm sure you can at least imagine it or imagine opening an old-school bottle of your favorite soda. Whatever. This book is about getting you past that moment of resistance and enjoying that sweet, sweet nectar called wealth. I wrote a lot of this book prior to writing the Preface, not because it's difficult, but because I wanted it to be right, not just for you, but for me, too. Apparently, a non-fiction book is supposed to have a great Preface to "Draw the Reader In". Again… Whatever. I didn't write this book because I need the money or require adoration and attention. (Actually, I've had to be extremely careful how I wrote this to keep my anonymity intact.) I wrote this book because I look around and see so many wonderful people on this planet struggling. People that don't deserve to struggle. Yes, some people just can't get out of their own way and will always struggle in life, they just love drama and mayhem. I hope that's not you, because I'm about to reveal how to become truly wealthy in every facet of your life. You will learn the differences between becoming rich and true wealth. Also, I'm apparently supposed to adhere to some word-count so that this book is long enough to be considered a "real book". I don't know about you, but although I like a good burger now and then, there's nothing like a great steak. Burgers are full of fillers with catsup, pickles, lettuce and mustard; and although you may enjoy eating it, afterwards you feel all bloated and gross. I would much rather offer you that really high-end steak-version of this book, minus the fillers, so that we can both get back to enjoying our wealth. (Oh, I see what this guy's doing, he's calling me wealthy before I'm there yet.) We are all wealthy in our own way, but our level of wealth is up to us. The by-product of what you are about to read should make you rich. Rich with knowledge, rich with money, rich with freedom, rich with understanding, rich with patience, rich with generosity, rich with faith… the list goes on. This is one of the few times I will reference riches, not because it's bad but because true wealth is a culmination of these riches and so much more. Also, using the word "rich" when referencing one's financial status is rather base and common. You will learn and appreciate this along your journey. So, you can stay in whatever situation you're in and have someone call the waahmbulance because they're frankly sick of listening to your griping and complaining, or you can do something, anything about it and start realizing your true wealth.

I really hope you enjoy this book, and that it allows you to realize all of the wonderful wealth that you so deserve in your life. This is not a "get rich quick" or "guaranteed to become a millionaire" book. As an example: I was once at an intersection waiting for the light to turn green and at the corner was a homeless person begging, holding up a sign about work and food. It dawned on me that even this guy has a job. If he doesn't show up to hold that sign, he won't get some sucker to give him their hard-earned money. So, you have to get out there at every opportunity to create and grow your wealth. This book may give you the knowledge and tools, but it's up to you to carry them out. I don't know your capabilities or lack thereof. I can only expect and see the best from you because I expect and see the best in everyone. This too, will become another part of your true wealth.

SERVICE THIS

By Liem Lionari

Chapter 1

What is the difference between a hundred thousand and a million? Zero. But wait, you might say, the difference is nine hundred thousand! But my response is if you add one zero to a hundred thousand, you have a million. It's that simple. So, if you sit down and look at your current wealth, how much do you have? Are you a hundredaire? Are you a thousandaire? Are you a ten-thousandaire or maybe a hundred-thousandaire? What are these words this guy's writing? Do they even exist? The short answer is, well maybe. But who in their right mind would brag about being any of these? Okay, maybe you might be proud of having a hundred thousand or a little more but you don't hear about these people on the news, or social media, or even through your friends or co-workers. But you do hear of people being millionaires and more. This is where I was, around the age of 28. I was fluctuating between the lower end of those maybe made-up words.

One evening after a long day of work I was pulling off my shoes, I looked down at my hands, my shirt and my filthy jeans; I stood and went to the mirror and thought how I was so exhausted I didn't want to shower, change and make myself dinner. My face and hair and arms and fingers were covered in various shades of saw dust and dirt. I looked at the person looking back at me and I wasn't happy. In that moment an overwhelming feeling of inspiration and excitement enveloped me. In that moment I became wealthy.

After my shower and while making dinner, my mind was so preoccupied by my new found wealth, I was dropping things and burned whatever it was I was cooking. It didn't matter, I was wealthy now and could afford it. I was too busy formulating and implementing my next steps and making notes; I could hardly write because my hand was shaking out of excitement. I had been a contractor for ten years. You get a job; you hurry up and do the job so that you don't have a job until you get another job. In the meantime, you're out collecting from people that owe you for a job you finished or you're out looking for more jobs. Ten years of this insanity and it finally dawned on me how stupid I've been! The service industry is simple. You do for others what most people don't know how to do or don't want to do for themselves. My service was contracting. I was good at it. It's hard work; there's ladders, big tools, small tools, power tools. It's a great way to get in shape, like ripped beyond what you thought was possible, good shape.

YOUR INSTANT WEALTH

Chapter 2

So, in that moment I realized that as good as I was at what I did, it wasn't making me wealthy. That is when I really understood wealth and how it is not measured by how much money is in your checking or savings account. Anyone that ever tells you that money does not buy you happiness has never truly had money. When you have money, you have freedom; and this freedom allows you to pursue other interests or hobbies that previously were unattainable to you due to a lack of time and/or money. Money buys you time, it opens doors, it serves you and if you're not careful; it will destroy you. After learning this through trial and error, life became quite simpler.

Who Is This Guy?

Before I share with you how to start adding zeros, you're probably wondering who I am and why you should read this book. I'm a high-school drop-out, (red flag: should probably stop reading), I probably made every single mistake possible for over a decade before becoming a millionaire, (Okay, maybe this guy learned something worth sharing). I can walk into any restaurant, shopping mall, public/private event or airport in any country and no one knows who I am. Total and complete ambiguity. (Damn, wealthy and he's basically a ghost? Cool).

LIEM LIONARI

WINDOW SHOPPING FOR FOOD

Chapter 3

I remember years ago before I became wealthy, my girlfriend (at the time) and I were at the grocery store. We were buying the essentials for the week, which was just that… weak. We were passing by the meat cases and stopped, both admiring all the different and wonderful kinds of steaks. We looked at each other and shook our heads, talking about how hopefully someday we'd buy one of those steaks and share it. It was not long after that my whole life changed. I was working long days and longer hours. My monthly (good) income was roughly $1,500. With rent, gas, food, utilities, cell phone, car insurance, etc. there wasn't much left. It was around this time that I became wealthy. I soon went from scratching out $1,500/month to making $15,000/week. I'm going to tell you exactly how.

SOMETHING I SHOULD MENTION

Chapter 4

So far you will notice that I have only mentioned the word wealth or wealthy. There is a real difference between riches and wealth. I have known and still know many rich people. Truly wealthy people have monetary riches but are wealthy in other unfathomable areas of their lives. One can be rich but lack good health. A friend of mine's best friend was dying of cancer and was worth $100,000,000. His friend was sitting with him in the hospital as he dozed in and out of consciousness. He had two grown children at home that wouldn't go and visit him, they were patiently awaiting his death to receive their inheritance. He stirred awake and in a moment of strength, reached over and grabbed my friend's arm, saying "I will give you all of my money, all of my everything if you can save me." My friend held his hand gently and said "I don't want your money but I wish I could save you." In a miraculous twist his friend's cancer went into remission and he lived for another ten years. His children weren't too happy and I'm sure there were some changes made to his will. One can be rich but have horrible family or friends. One can be rich but be a mean person. Wealthy people understand the difference and do their best to uplift those around them, even the rich. Wealthy people don't act more important than those around them, have huge egos or expand their wealth by taking advantage of others. Most wealthy people strive to surround themselves with other like-minded people. They seek each other out for philanthropic purposes, discussing business ventures, seeking advice, leisure activities and hobbies, etc. Wealthy people are no different than anyone else, they just have a lot of money, a LOT. They are (mostly) also kind, intelligent, giving and willing to mentor those around them. I, personally, don't treat my domestic assistant or driver any different than if the Pope walked through my front door today. One time a friend asked me "What's a domestic assistant and why do you have one?" I simply said that she cooks, cleans, takes care of my pets and lives in my home. Then I asked him "Why don't you have one?" He then asked why I have a driver? I said "Because I can get a lot of work done during what I call 'windshield time'; with emails, phone calls, texting, etc. This way, when my day is complete, I can pursue my other more enjoyable interests." Then I asked him "Why don't you have one?" Wealthy people realize early on that time is one of the most precious commodities. In this book you will learn that work only has to be a four-letter-word if you allow it to be. You will learn that it's fun to have fun and how to finally have fun, and that although your business might seem paramount, family and friends, creativity, vacations and hobbies are extremely important as well.

STATISTICS AND SKIP-AHEAD SYNDROME

Chapter 5

So, you've read this much and if you'd prefer, skip ahead to chapter whatever and learn how to become wealthy. I have no idea what chapter that is yet because by now, you may have realized that I'm not writing this book as the vast majority are conventionally written. We live in a world where most people have a short-attention span. With the internet, social media, smart phones and tablets; people are in such a hurry to hurry up and learn a whole bunch of even less, I'm actually impressed you've made it this far. I'm even more impressed that I've made it this far writing it. Part of the reason is because I've never written a book before and I absolutely know it won't be a long one. That's great news for you and this is where I make up a few statistics that should be rather close to the truth. Once I explain to you how to become wealthy, (assuming you've bought this book and have read this far) I'm guessing maybe 20% of you will actually do anything with the knowledge, herein. Of that 20%, maybe only 2% will follow through far enough and become wealthy. Did I piss you off? Good. There's an old saying about giving people fish and will they eat for a day, but if you teach them to fish, they eat for a lifetime. If 100,000 people buy my book on sale from $24.95 for only $9.99, I just grossed almost $1 Million and why should I care what you do after that? Did that piss you off again? Even better. But, hopefully (for your sake) that 2% of you out there will become wealthy, too. If I could do that for you, (all joking aside) it would truly be my honor and pleasure to be that person whom guided you along in your journey to wealth. I sincerely want 1000% of all of you that are reading this to become wealthy… more than just rich. Come on this journey with me of adding zeros. I was a zero for too many years. I will never forget it. I shared these statistics not because their true, but to light a fire under your feet.

ANONYMITY AND WHY IT'S IMPORTANT TO ME

Chapter 6

I may be the one person that changes your life in an indescribably positive way but you'll never know who I am. I spent several hours debating what my 'pen name' should be. It isn't a real name, or at least not my real name but it should hold value to you. I like being able to go anywhere and not have an entourage of people following me, taking my picture, wanting an autograph, judging how I'm dressed, who I'm with, etc. Could you imagine being a movie or music star, a pro athlete or famous whoever? The people in my circles speak of this often and we all agree how miserable this must be. These famous people have sold their souls for fame and fortune. Trust me, it's much, much nicer to have the fortune without the fame. The interesting part is, when you're out in a public place and you run into someone wealthy that you know or even don't know; but you know and they know that you are one of them and they are one of you, there's this indiscernible nod or look, like being a member of this private club that exists but doesn't. This club is out there with open memberships and I'm going to tell you how to join.

Why Am I Doing This

I'm writing this book because too many people need to get back to what's most important: YOU. There's no mistake that I am referring to you as a 'what' and not a 'who'. Who you are starts with what you are. Only you can truly control your financial outcome in life. Only you can be a good spouse or parent. Only you can stop being lazy. Only you can create a legacy for your family. Only you can get up every day and implement these steps and become wealthy. Fear should be your fuel, not your reason for failure. You should be more fearful of staying where you are in life because you know that all too well. How's that working out for you? I know you must be thinking that this guy's not really very nice. Did you ever have a coach in high-school that would ride you like a cheap stolen bicycle? I read somewhere that a good coach wins games but a great one changes lives. Yeah, maybe what I say in here might offend some of you, but it takes busy-ness to have a business. So, get busy. I know a lot of people that miss that coach; they can't remember their other teachers, but they remember and respect that coach.

LEGAL MUMBO JUMBO (MUST READ)

Chapter 7

First and foremost, I am NOT an Attorney, Lawyer, Barrister, Accountant, CPA, Licensed Insurance Agent, any type of Agent, Financial Planner, Wealth Management Advisor, Licensed Securities Adviser or Trader, Banker, nor do I have my MBA or any other type of proper education giving me the official capacity to advise anyone on how to set up a business entity, bank accounts, insurance, etc. I know what I did to set up my businesses and personally found it to be rather simple as each one only took a few days. If you don't know how to do something, there's always the internet that will guide you in finding the correct person or businesses that will help you legally set up your business. Now that we have that behind us, let's get started!

SO EASY IT'S DUMB

Chapter 8

To recap briefly, I had been working ten long years as a contractor. Hurry up and finish a job so I no longer have a job… The moment I became wealthy had nothing to do with my checking account, it had everything to do with my approach. I realized that I was wearing too many hats. Last time I felt around, there was only one of me. (After a big steak, there's a little more of me, but still just one of me!) This is when, staring in the mirror, I realized that after all of these years I'd been running my business very wrong. Instead of concentrating on the negative, we'll skip that and move ahead to what's right; how to do it properly, why you should do it this certain way and when is the best time to get started.

As I mentioned before, the service industry is designed around providing a service for people that don't have the skills, tools or desire to do it themselves and it is extremely lucrative. "Sure, I can shovel snow off of my driveway or cut my own grass, but why not pay the neighbor kid up the street $20 while I sit back and watch the game? Easy. Come to think of it, there's a flyer on my door offering deck staining and it could use another few coats. When did my stucco start to crack? I need to call that guy that my buddy at work knows…" All of these people are specialized in certain trades or services. All they want to do is get up every single day and go to work. Most of them are very family oriented, extremely hard-working, artisans of their craft but not so great at business. Once I realized this, (myself included) I became wealthy.

THIS IS THE GOOD STUFF

Chapter 9

Most people believe (or possibly use the excuse driven by fear) that you need a lot of money to start a service business. Not true in most cases. The first thing you can do prior to starting a service business is to do a bit of research in your area (or market) and find out if it's a viable business. Will this business thrive? Example: You want to open a deep-sea fishing guide business in the middle of the desert. I'm going to guess epic fail. You live on or near a beach town somewhere and you have the same idea. Okay, that's more viable but how many other companies offer the same? Is the market saturated? Do you have a bigger or nicer boat? Do you have a boat at all? These are the questions you have to ask yourself and others. But let's say that you find out there are only a few other companies doing this and there's a decent demand. So, you rush out and buy a new shiny boat (with a loan from the bank) WRONG and fill it full of fishing rods and life jackets and other stuff you think you need (that you paid for with your credit card) WRONG and now you're in business! WRONG. Guess again, you're not in business, you're in debt, and a LOT of it.

Here's the correct approach in this scenario: You did your homework and there's a good demand for deep-sea fishing guides from what you can tell by researching a few things on the web, but how old is that info? Is it weeks old? Years old? Decades old? This is when you actually start your business. This new venture may last a few hours or multiple decades. The next step will be for you to start marketing your new company. It's okay if you get business and you don't even own a boat. This is where the magic starts to happen. You can run a few social media ads, put out flyers, even talk to your co-workers or friends and ask them when they'd like to hire your company to take them out on a fantastic deep-sea fishing trip! Your guides know all the best spots!

Now I'm going to stop for a moment and point out a few key things that you may or may not have noticed. Did you notice that I referred to your business and not you? Your business will take your clients (customers) out on the boat, not you. I said when, not if, your clients wanted to go on this excursion. This kind of mindset if extremely important in business. Did you notice that you have guides taking your clients out, not you? This is because you don't even have to own a boat to operate this business. You're the owner not the guide. You live on or near the beach, remember? You're not the only one with a boat. There are a few people out there that would love nothing more than to make money showing people how and where to fish. All you have to do is charge X amount to your clients, pay the guide X amount less and you keep the difference. The best part is you keep marketing this until you have five or ten or twenty guides and now, you're making X amount off of each one. So, instead of you rushing out and buying a shiny new boat and supplies that will only put you in a huge amount of debt and accommodate only one guide (probably you because you can't afford to hire an actual guide), you invested a small amount on marketing and are making bank off of multiple guides and they're using their own boats! Boom!

Okay, so I'm making this sound so easy, right? Yes, it is that easy. When I realized this, that's when I went from $1,500/month to $15,000/week (and just wait until $15,000/week seems like a joke). The really important part is that you HAVE to make all of your (in this case) 'Guides' sub-contractors, meaning they have to perform work for you as non-employees. You have your business entity with insurance, worker's comp, etc. and they have their own business entity with insurance, worker's comp, etc. Before they perform any work for your company, they have to sign a Non-Employee Sub-Contractors Agreement and a Work Safety Agreement. You must charge your clients by the fishing trip, flat-rate and you pay your sub-contractor guides by the job, NOT by the hour. Then your accountant or tax advisor will take it from there. It is paramount that you and the people that your sub-contractors ALWAYS carry insurance. In this scenario, let's say your client is out having a great time fishing; then they hook their nipple, now they need a nipple-ectomy which requires a trip to the ER. This doesn't seem good at all. It would be much worse if your company or your sub-contractor's company doesn't have insurance. Very bad, indeed. Obviously, your client would have to sign a waiver prior to even stepping on a boat. This is a very good reason to have a legal advisor/attorney write up a solid contract for you.

Now, I'm not saying everyone should run out and start a deep-sea fishing guide business. Frankly, I wish I had thought of another example as it's not easy to repeatedly type "deep-sea fishing guide business". Either way, this is applicable in most any type of service business. You can start a lawn service business, snow removal, deck/fence staining, power washing, painting, stucco, tile, window washing, house cleaning, window tinting, paint-less dent repair (PDR), junk removal, dump trailer rentals, post-construction clean-up, landscaping, aeration, sprinkler winterization/de-winterization, pest control, windshield, auto-body repair, carpet cleaning, gutter installation, dog washing/grooming, pooper scooper, etc. The list goes on...

The key is to have enough subs so that you NEVER actually have to do this work yourself. You must have redundancy in your workforce. There's an old saying: buyers are liars and workers don't show up. Always have more subs than you need. After some time, you will find out who's reliable and who isn't. You can't fire them because they don't actually work for you; they do sub-contract work for your company. All you have to do is stop using them, tell them that you don't have work for them right now; but never delete them from your contact list because you never know when you'll need them out of pure desperation (unless they do something extremely bad like stealing, drunk/high on the job or rude to your client.)

Now you may ask, which one on the list is best for me? Only you can answer that based on where in the world you live, the climate (both literally and fiscally) and interestingly enough, what flips your switch? Where do your interests lie? Even though you won't actually be doing the work, you will need to know something about what service you're providing. Boots on the ground is the only way to learn. Even if you shadow your subs for a while. You need to know what you're talking about when speaking to your clients. One good source is to call a rep that supplies your product. Let's say you have a carpet installation company. There's a store where you buy your carpet that your subs (installers) will need the carpet from. You pay for the carpet, pad, tack strip, seam tape, glue (I'm making this up, I've no idea what you'd need); but before you buy any of this, you'll open an account with Whatever Named Carpet Supply. They will assign you with a rep. Your rep will set you up with a charge account (assuming you have good credit) or what is called a Cash Account, meaning you still get a discount for purchasing there but you have to pay before they give you any carpet or supplies. This is all set up under your company name. Now, let's say you have a client that is asking all sorts of questions about different types of carpet; colors, strands, stain resistance, whatever. You have no idea how to answer these questions or all of them. So, you tell your client that there are some new products out (you're not lying because there's always new products out) and tell them that you'll follow up right away because you want to make sure and give them the best product for their needs that suites their budget. Now you call or text your rep with those questions and relay the response back to your client. Your rep's job is to make sure that you're selling jobs. Your rep gets paid based upon all of their clients doing well. If you do well, your rep does well. Also, if you need help finding good sub-contractors, your rep in whatever trade you're in will be a great source for connecting you to a team he trusts and has been vetted by others. Another option is when while driving, you see a team of workers performing the same line of work you offer or are interested in starting, stop, get out and exchange information. Ask them if they do sub-work. Almost all will say "Yes". Create a file of these teams and label them based on their trade or trades. Go to stores where they buy their supplies, make sure to go early in the morning because you are more likely to find the good teams that are willing to wake early and be there when the store opens. This speaks volumes about you and the team you are looking to add to your sub-contractors list.

STAY DESIRABLE

Chapter 10

There's a secret sauce that will help you when running your service business. DON'T BE AVAILABLE. You are the owner, act like it. You're important. Un-important people are always available. Look at your phone and let it ring until it goes to voicemail. Make a note of who called and when, then call or text them back a short while later. Once you get to a certain level, hire an outside source to answer your business number and only let a few people have your private personal number.

BRUSH YOUR TEETH AND GET DRESSED

Chapter 11

One of the most important details in business is your appearance. If you dress like a busted fool, you're not going to get the job. If all you have is one nice pair of jeans, a polo shirt and shoes; then that's what you're wearing every single day when you meet your clients. Once you get your first check, go shopping. One of the most important items of all is your shoes. People will notice your shoes. If you're dressed well but wearing beat up old shoes, you will be judged. Another item of mention is your smell. If you smoke anything prior to meeting a client, you will be judged. If your personal hygiene is not at its absolute best: fail. People don't want to smell you unless you smell clean, and drinking or smoking prior to meeting a client is one of the absolute worst things you could do. Make sure to be clean-shaven or at least a trimmed beard and your hair should be well-managed. I've had so many clients in the past complement me on my appearance when I visit their project. They mentioned that the last person showed up dirty, wild hair, missing teeth, smelled of marijuana and/or alcohol. I have a 90% close rate for a reason. If you are missing a tooth or need dental work, that is another one of your top priorities needing attention. People in general are mean and judgmental. I don't know what your current path is in life and I don't know what led you to reading this book. What I do know is that bad teeth can lead to a multitude of other health issues and should be a priority in everyone's life. It's actually possible to have issues with your teeth and not even know it. Just because you don't have pain doesn't mean everything is okay. Regular check-ups will help prevent issues in the future.

NETWORKING

Chapter 12

Here's one of the best parts about owning a service business. You actually get to make people happy to see you! There are a core group of other business owners that love to network. The best one is Real Estate Agents. For the most part, whatever your service business is, a real estate agent probably knows someone that knows someone that needs your service. The more real estate agents you can network with, the more work you will get. All you do is give them your card and tell them that you'd like to have some of their cards so that you can refer your clients, friends and family when they are ready to buy or sell. Another great source is roofing contractors. Let's say you own a paint-less dent repair business. When there's a hail storm, a roofer is super busy replacing damaged roofs. You've networked with their company by offering to refer roof jobs to them and they refer dent jobs to you. Networking really pays off if approached and exercised properly. One definite word of caution is to never (at least in the beginning) take on really large projects. General contractors are always looking for subs to do work for them. Now you're sub-contracting under a general contractor as a sub-contractor with sub-contractors. This can become a very messy cocktail, indeed. Let's say you're doing this huge job for some GC and you're going to make all this money. Your subs are almost finished with the job and you've been paying them draws and buying materials for over a month; now suddenly the GC decides that you've taken too long or they don't like your work or whatever other made-up reason and they bounce you off the job. You tell them they owe you all this money and the GC just smiles and tells you to sue them! So, let's recap briefly: You've paid your subs, you've bought all of this material and supplies and the job has been going on for a month or so. This GC knows that you don't have the horse-power to sue them because they will just have their expensive attorneys keep you in court for months or years. All they have to do is hire another company to finish your job for pennies on the dollar and move on. You would not believe how many of these stories I've heard through the years. It happens more often than you'd think. My suggestion is to never put yourself in this situation in the first place. Always work directly with the owner, whether you're doing work on their home, auto, building, etc. People tend to pay you when you know where they live. Many years ago, early one morning, I parked my truck in front a client's driveway so that (this time) he would remember to grab his checkbook on his way to work. I just sat there, politely smiling until he went back inside and wrote me a check. In business and in life, sometimes you have to educate people on how you expect to be treated.

SOMETHING FOR NOTHING AND THE SNOWBALL EFFECT

Chapter 13

There will always be clients that expect something for nothing. That's okay, to a degree. There's the 'while you're here, could you just…' client; and as long as it's not too much, then do it. It will bode well for you in the long run. If it's a lot, then just politely tell them you'd be happy to provide an additional quote for the change order. Most people don't trust contractors or anyone in the service industry. Always go the extra mile within reason. Let them think that they're slightly taking advantage of you or that they're just simply getting extra good service. They will tell their family and friends about your company and how well they were treated. Also, this is a secret insurance policy, just in case something isn't perfect with the rest of the project. Of course, you'll make it right, but this helps a lot if you've already added a little extra freebie on to the job. I usually have my teams go out of their way to ask the client if they can do something extra that they noticed should be fixed or corrected, for free. This is just the right thing to do for the client and also excellent marketing for your company. In addition, you will absolutely set your company apart from the competition that always try to chisel their clients over small change orders. Just remember, there's a delicate balance, you don't want to give away the farm.

TWO FULL-TIME JOBS

Chapter 14

In the preface I mentioned "whambulance", kind of a dick move but hopefully it got your attention. No one, and I mean no one really wants to listen to you complaining about your current job all the time. Not your significant other, your co-workers, your friends or family, no one. I can tell you from experience, if you're not happy with your current job, now you have two full-time jobs; your current job and looking for a new job that hopefully you will like. Nobody wants to hear your negativity. "But I thought you wanted me to start service businesses?" you may ask. Well, that's up to you. Either way, you still need to make a living while you're building your businesses. Remove negativity from your life and you will be amazed at what and whom it attracts in the most positive ways. I, personally can't work for anyone. Yes, I own companies that do work for clients, but I'm incapable of punching a clock and being a yes-man. I'm not saying this is bad for those that do, it's just not in my DNA. I look at companies and am fascinated by how I would run them, what their marketing strategies look like, how I would do it differently, or how I could emulate theirs if I'm impressed. You will start to see life and business with new eyes and realize that negativity and complaining will only attract negative energy vampires. A friend once told me that fundamentally there are two kinds of people in this world: Givers and Takers. He then paused and said: "your girlfriend is a Taker and I wouldn't be your friend if I didn't tell you." I was mad at him for telling me. Not because he was wrong, but because I was so embarrassed that it was that obvious. This was another pivotal moment in my life. I learned that a lot of a person's success is dependent upon whom they surround themselves with. I was with someone that had nothing to give other than her looks and a big bag full of drama. This opened my eyes to all of these like-kind people in my life and quickly grew to have an incurable allergy to them. Fortunately, and unfortunately, we are all judged in every facet of our lives; especially concerning to whom our friends are. Be cognizant of this, as it could make or break you, especially in business.

REMEDIES INSTEAD OF ENEMIES

Chapter 15

There are a lot of wonderful people in this world, don't get me wrong. I don't want you to think this book is all about doom and gloom when it comes to the masses. I'm a 'glass-half' full person and always will be. A while back, I was at a big-box membership store standing in line with one item in my hand and after waiting for what seemed like forever because the place was packed, this kind woman in front of me noticed that I was holding only one item. She had a huge shopping cart, filled to the brim with her items and offered for me to go ahead of her. I politely declined and after thanking her, explained that it wouldn't be fair as she had been waiting in line as long as I had. She insisted, I acquiesced and stepped past her in line. After I finished with my quick purchase, they ran her membership card, I quickly ran my card and paid for her items and walked away. Once I got to my truck, I stopped to answer a brief phone call and just as I finished up the woman that allowed me to jump ahead in line was pushing her cart towards me. She was in tears and paused as she approached me. I said "Are you okay?" She said, "Thank you for what you did back there. Life has been very difficult lately and you have restored my faith in humanity." I said "It was nothing more than my honor and pleasure." What I learned in that moment is that no matter what's going on with you, there's always someone else that's got theirs going on with them. We all need each other in some form or fashion. We should be remedies instead of enemies. I would much rather do the right thing and be taken advantage of by someone than live my life being fearful or untrusting towards others. I truly believe that we will be blessed through giving. When I was young, I was painfully shy. It took me many years to break out of that shell. In business, shyness is not an option. You have to show strength even when you're not certain. You have to exude knowledge without all of the facts. You will get the facts because you're in charge and you have to guide your businesses like the helm of a ship; and you will learn the most during rough seas. You will recognize those whom are not healthy for you or your business; whether it be clients, friends or even family members. Remember that WHO you are starts with WHAT you are. It truly was my honor and pleasure to return a kind gesture for that lady. When you are in this position soon, you will enjoy the same realization. There is no price-tag that one could attach to that feeling because it was no different than how I felt when she offered for me to go ahead of her.

ALWAYS BE THE DUMBEST PERSON IN THE ROOM

Chapter 16

I've often said that the best way for me to make the best decisions is to ensure sure I'm surrounded by the smartest people. I could just stop here but this truly is important. Especially when you're starting your first business, if you're the smartest person (or even worse, if you THINK you're the smartest person), then you've just set yourself up for a big 'ole bucket full of failure. You may succeed eventually, but you will fail many times until you get there. In order to skip through that heart-ache and pain, make sure to seek out people in your industry that have been through the tough times, have made the mistakes. Ask questions, people LOVE to talk about themselves because we are all so ego-centric. Just look up the value of any popular social media website/app and research how many "users" they have. If you are the smartest one in your group, then you're in the wrong group. In order to run a successful company, you should be surrounding yourself with even more successful people than yourself. It's a journey, not a competitive destination.

THE LINT SCREEN EFFECT

Chapter 17

Someone once told me that "Poor performance is proceeded by poor planning" and "If you fail to plan, you've planned to fail". Then again that same person also said "Don't sweat the petty sh*t, but make sure to pet the sweaty sh*t". I think that's a good one, but not 100% sure how to wrap my head around the last part. Either way, it's extremely important to plan ahead, which will allow your business to have every opportunity for success. The best way to plan ahead is to educate yourself before you start anything. So, what's the 'Lint Screen Effect'? Many years ago, before I had a house manager, I was always in a hurry to do everything. Hurry up and go to work, find work, do paperwork, cook, clean, find even more work, chase people down that owe me money and the worst of the worst of all that is unholy… laundry. I absolutely despise doing laundry. And for a guy that loves to buy clothes, laundry is a real and present problem that never ends. I prefer not to wear the same clothes often; therefore, my laundry mountain is unlike most. So, this brings us back to the Lint Screen Effect. Here I am, rushing through life, always in a hurry. Every time I did laundry, I had to clean the dryer lint screen, otherwise my clothes wouldn't dry. I spent years hurriedly trying to clean the lint screen in my dryer with much frustration, smearing my finger across it and finally getting a small piece to come off. It was so incredibly maddening! This literally went on once a week for years. I even contemplated a redesign so that us mere mortals could live our lives in harmony and finally achieve world peace. Then one day, it happened… my girlfriend walked in to the laundry room and stood there watching me struggling and (as usual) hurriedly trying to remove the lint from the dryer screen.

She said "why are you cussing at the dryer?" I turned slightly and said "what kind of idiot would design such a stupid contraption that won't allow you to clean the lint screen!?" She just quietly chuckled and reached around me and touched her index finger on my wet laundry sitting in the dryer. She then ran her damp finger across the lint screen in a circular motion and by some sort of miraculous voodoo, all of the lint was magically gone and stuck to her finger! She then reached down and flicked it into the trash can. I looked at her… my head spinning off of its axis. I'd spent year after year dreading laundry day, not just because of the lint screen but also because of the lint screen. I was in so much of a hurry all the time, I never stopped to plan how I was going to do the necessary things I needed to do to be efficient. I looked at her and said "Just like that?" She walked away shaking her head, mumbling "It's like something." Many years later when I sometimes walk by the laundry room, I cringe. Maybe it's laundry PTSD, who knows, but I'm still thankful for that experience because it taught me another valuable lesson; in life and in business, if you're always in a hurry to hurry up and hurry, you're only setting yourself up for failure. Sit down, breathe, plan. Educate yourself on how to find solutions. There are never problems, just poor planning. Plan properly and you will succeed, if nothing else in learning how to plan more proficiently in the future. I'm so excited for you to learn this if you learn nothing else in this book. Like I said before, it's the rough seas that teach you the most in life and in business while at the helm. Always the Captain, never the First Mate.

WHO DOESN'T LOVE A GOOD TREASURE HUNT?

Chapter 18

In 1794 – 1795 the United States minted the first half-dollar. It was called the Flowing Hair and contained 89.24% silver, with a troy ounce silver weight of .3868. From 1796 – 1807 they minted the Draped Bust. From 1807 – 1839 they minted the Capped Bust. From 1839 – 1891 they minted the Seated Liberty. From 1892 – 1915 they minted the Barber. From 1916 – 1947 they minted the Walking Liberty. From 1948 – 1963 they minted the Franklin. In 1964 the United States minted the Kennedy. All roughly with the same 90% silver content and troy ounce weight. From 1965 – 1970 they minted the Kennedy half dollar with only 40% silver and by 1971 all silver was removed. So, what does this have to do with a treasure hunt and more importantly what does this have to do with your book? I thought it was over, done, finished? It has everything to do with this book. But, first, I want to talk about the treasure hunt… You see, most people don't know this, but you can get those for free (well, almost free, they will cost you fifty cents). All you have to do is go to your local bank and order a box of half dollars. They are $500/box. Once you get them home, remove them from the wrappers and look to see if they are silver. A quick way is to check the edge; if it doesn't have copper, then it's probably silver. Then check the date. If it's prior to 1971 it's either 40% silver or if it's prior to 1965, It's 90% silver. Why am I telling you this and why should you do this? Well, if you paid roughly $10.00 for this book and find find a few of these coins (depending on the year), then you just basically paid for this book. Not bad. The other reason is simple. Unless you're reading this book on your smart phone, tablet or computer; put your electronic devices down. Walk away. After reading this book, do something, anything. Someone recently said to me that the best position your body can be in is your next one. In other words, move. Your mind will thank you. I don't need to buy half dollars and go on a treasure hunt, but I do sometimes. I have many of them and if you find some that are rare or in uncirculated condition, they are worth quite a bit. But still, that's not my point. Get off of your smart devices, they are making you dumb. My friends and I were recently joking that if we were visited by some intelligent life, they would wonder why our heads are bowed, worshipping these devices. Just look around the next time you're at a restaurant; the whole family looking at their phones and even their little toddler usually has some sort of tablet to keep them "quiet". Truly sad. But let's get back to the treasure hunt! Why should you do this? Well, its actually great fun. You can do it solo, have your family and friends join in, but make sure that the rule is, finders' keepers. I once bought $2000.00 worth and found nothing. Then again, I once found a dozen or more in one box. Mostly you'll find silver Kennedy half dollars but once in a while you'll find a Franklin and rarely a Walking Liberty. Anything prior to those minting years would be epic in my opinion. The main reason for this exercise is simple and it has nothing to do with getting rich. It does have everything to do with wealth, though. This will get you out of your present mind-set, make you think differently about your time and literally money. Make sure not to wear gloves, you'll be cussing at me later but it's a good lesson in how filthy money can be. The wealth part comes in once you find one. After your heart rate slows back down (it truly is exciting, at least the first few times), what will you do with it? Are you going to keep it? Put it on your desk or in an obvious spot to remind you about this book and the inception of your true wealth? Will you sell it? (I truly hope not). There is no wrong answer, really. It's just a simple way to force your mind into thinking differently and creating new patterns; or at least redirecting your current patterns. Statistically, you may have had one of them pass through your hands and not even known, but now you do. Or, maybe you did know but didn't care. Either way, now you have a reason to care because it should garner more value to you than just from a numismatic standpoint. The best way to get rid of that old lawn mower is to put it out on the street with a sign that says $10.

Someone will either come along and buy it or more than likely, steal it. Either way, problem solved. But if you put it out with a "free" sign, it will probably sit there for days. Your mistake? Not giving it value. Another interesting statistic; if you bought this book (or any book), instead of it being given to you, even though you paid roughly $10 for it (you used to be able to buy a burger and fries for that), you are more likely to read it and actually follow along and retain what you're reading. If it was given to you or you stole it, statistically you will not read it nor ever finish it, much less retain what you've read or follow through with its content. Giving value to something invokes a sense of ownership, responsibility and most importantly, a sense of self-worth. And we all know that self-worth is ego-driven. So, now you know why everyone loves a good treasure hunt! It has nothing to do with riches and everything to do with wealth.

WHAT'S IN A NAME

Chapter 19

Don't forget, my name is not Liem Lionari, but there is great value in this pen name I chose. I briefly mentioned it prior, but let's call it the hidden Easter Egg in my book. I challenge you to figure it out, and once you do, I think you will appreciate it.

GIVING THANKS

Chapter 20

I genuinely appreciate you reading this book. I sincerely hope that on some level it helped you on your path to true wealth. I will not, nor cannot guarantee that you will become rich or wealthy as a by-product from reading this book. It's hardly a book really, it's more of a short-story-long. Either way, it means a lot to me that you have read it. I decided that if only one copy sells, I will consider it a win. If I can change only one person's life for the better, all the hours I spent writing this will be worth it.

You're shopping cart is full (of broken dreams and disappointment), I'm in line behind you, this single item in hand (a simple book that packs a punch). The next move is up to you.

www.ingramcontent.com/pod-product-compliance
Lightning Source LLC
Chambersburg PA
CBHW030102230526
45471CB00003B/1212